Contents

Introduction		v
Chapter One:	Success With Employees Within Your Four Walls	1
Chapter Two:	Leadership Within Your Four Walls	12
Chapter Three:	Accountability and Responsibility Within Your Four Walls	33
Chapter Four:	Training Within Your Four Walls	46
Chapter Five:	Develop Managers Within Your Four Walls	55
Chapter Six:	Reflections on Leadership Within Your Four Walls	62

Introduction

Leading and managing within the four walls of quick-service restaurants is very different from managing a typical corporate office, branch, division, product line, or region. Customer service and product satisfaction aren't delayed responses in quick service. Feedback is immediate. In many cases it's nonverbal but not invisible to the leader and service team who are paying attention. People are very particular about service and quality when it comes to their food. The bottom-line impact that comes from pleasing customers, or displeasing them, is seen immediately. But the decision to please or displease customers was made long before they entered your restaurant. Revenue loss was just about etched in stone the first time your product or service was delivered with a quality lower than what customers remembered seeing advertised. No matter what you want to say about corporate, the bottom-line is: "at the end of the day, you're responsible for what happens within your four walls." Success, increased pay, added responsibilities, bonuses, and the sheer satisfaction of delivering your product and service as promised are all within your control. You choose, every day you open your doors for business, whether or not your restaurant will be successful.

I know that was a little tart for an introduction. I'd suggest you find a place to sit, fasten your seat belt, and set aside your ego and emotions, because this won't be sugarcoated, watered-down, or lost in translation. Within these pages lies the answer to that deep, nagging question that you dare not say aloud except to your closest confidant: "What the hell does corporate want me to do, make profit out of thin air, with this labor, with this equipment, in this neighborhood, or with the constant changes in how we do business?" Yes, that is one long question, but you have said it more than once. From this day forward, you will be leading the charge and shamelessly accountable for each success or failure within your four walls.

After working many years in the fast food industry, from entry level to senior leadership, it's obvious to me that there is a need for a book that addresses leadership and what general managers face within the four walls of their restaurants.

There is also a need for a book that's in fast-food industry language and is a fast read that will allow busy quick-service restaurant managers to immediately identify and address the various strengths, weaknesses, opportunities, and challenges of leading and managing in this industry.

In quick-service restaurants managers need to lead and to overcome the obstacles and barriers that occur within their four walls on a daily basis. Because many restaurant general managers grew up in the fast food industry, they frequently carry previous managers' leadership and management DNA and, therefore, end up with the same results. That's not always a bad thing. However, too many times they fail to recognize how to lead a restaurant team to become a high-performing one. When managers have their own brands that are finely threaded with signature training, productive mentoring, and personally and incrementally developed capabilities of leading and managing, their restaurants have greater potential to excel in service, quality, sales, and profits. With this type of manager there are rarely days, weeks, or months where the results are below par. Actually, they are more likely to be market leaders.

As restaurant leaders, it's important to have a solid foundation within the four walls of your restaurant. When talking about a solid foundation, we're talking about your actions as the leader of your team. As the leader, your actions and activities are setting standards, whether good or bad. Whether your restaurant is Wendy's, KFC, McDonald's, Steak 'n Shake, Chipotle, or some other chain, your company has standards that have to be consistent across the country and, in some instances, even the world. All have procedures and policies requiring consistency in the building of their brands. And they all provide processes designed to assist you in being successful at leading and managing within your four walls.

I'm an avid lover of professional basketball. I see many parallels between restaurant management and basketball. There's one thing in particular that I find fascinating about the game—the role of the point guard. When a team has a skilled point guard, it usually finishes in the top eight in its league and moves on to the playoffs. The team may or may not win the championship, but it's successful in driving the next year's profits, because the attendance will increase based on the buzz about the team's proven ability to make the playoffs. As the leader of your restaurant, you're the team's point guard, and the ball is always in your court. Your ball-handling (leadership and management) skills will allow your team to win game after game, season after season. In other words, your restaurant team will succeed day after day and be poised for growing sales and profits year after year. When the ball is in the manager's court, the manager is laying a foundation that will allow him or her to compete in this competitive quick-service industry. By handling the leadership ball correctly on your court (within your four walls), you ensure that your restaurant will be successful.

Leadership is a constant responsibility in upper management, human resources, and even among the employees—yes, the employees. We can't escape being leaders within the four walls of our restaurants.

Successful leaders in quick-service restaurants understand their responsibility for training and developing a team that will be successful in growing sales, which leads to higher profit margins, higher bonuses, and, if your employer offers them, stock options. The experienced leader of a restaurant knows that setting the example is the only way to influence positive behavior and high performance.

I've known and trained many successful restaurant general managers throughout the country, and over the years these people have made their marks by consistently setting the example through their leadership. Successful restaurant general managers know that the key to developing individuals is to consistently recognizing performance and to consistently train. These individuals are the building blocks of successful teams. Successful restaurant general managers don't blame the negative performance of their restaurants on things that are out of their control, such as advertising, economy, or the workforce. They know that if they have control within their four walls, the competitors surrounding their restaurants will be watching them grow sales, even in the toughest of times.

As we move into the core subject matter, I want to emphasize a couple of points about this book. It has short chapters that are easy to read. We'll be discussing five concepts of leading within your four walls. Each chapter will have a story that will explain one of the concepts and deal with many situations occurring today within your four walls. At the end of each chapter there will be questions for you to answer and consider. It's my hope that your thoughtful attention to what you read in this book will lead to change that is beneficial for you, your team, your customers, and your company. Everyone is a winner in one-way or another! Within your four walls, it's your court, your game, and your team. Play and lead to win!

Chapter One

Success With Employees Within Your Four Walls

Leading within your four walls is all about your employees. There isn't a basketball, football, or soccer team that can win with just one player dominating the game. When the players on the team are not filling their prescribed roles and flowing with one another that team will lose the game, and the next year's attendance will decline, just like sales in a restaurant.

In top-performing quick-service restaurants, the successful leader's team will go out of its way to reach whatever goal or milestone the leader has set. There is a misconception that in fast food the employees work for the company, but this is so far from the reality. Employees work for their immediate supervisor within the four walls of the restaurant and will follow that supervisor's lead. This means they all work for the restaurant general manager.

Most restaurant general managers are good at getting results, but most results are unsustainable, especially if they're achieved through dispassionate management practices and intimidating the employees. When this happens, you can count on the results having peaks and valleys, because managers are muscling the results rather than getting them through leading, motivating, training, and developing their teams. Unless this concept is grasped and put into practice, these managers will continuously struggle, suffer from stress, and be doomed to operational stagnation. They will simply fail to accomplish the goals and objectives they agreed to achieve when they sought out the leading role within their four walls.

A general manager who's a strong leader will achieve results that continue throughout his or her tenure, regardless of whether that manager is left at a particular restaurant or moved to several restaurants; the results will be the same wherever he or she is planted.

As the general manager, leading your team has to be your number one priority. You're influencing the behaviors of people who work with you; your actions must match what you're trying to convey to your employee. Setting examples in every facet of your operation is the key to influencing others within the four walls of the restaurant. You get in return what you give and display. As the general manager, you can help the team be successful by providing them with knowledge and tools to achieve 100 percent, perfected customer satisfaction by delivering great service and quality products in a clean and safe environment from open to close (or around the clock in always-open operations).

Let's take a look at the point about being the example. The only way to be sure your team will become a high performing one is to understand that they will do as you do, no matter what you say you do. For example, if you never praise your team, they won't praise each other, and their attitude will trickle down to every customer service point and affect how they serve and treat customers.

We often wonder how some restaurant managers can have turnover below 50 percent while others have well above 300 percent. The difference is that one manager has the employees working for him or her, and the other has employees working with him or her. These two different leadership styles yield entirely different results.

Managers, who have employees working with them, always look in the mirror and place themselves in their employees' shoes. These managers continuously ask themselves a litany of questions: Am I being fair when providing coaching? Do I show respect to my employees by saying such simple things as please and thank you? Do I recognize my employees as members of a team and as individuals? Am I giving employees the knowledge and tools they need to be successful? Am I creating a culture within my four walls that replicates the way I want the team to treat customers?

By putting yourself in the shoes of your employees, you're saying to them, "You are my most important assets." Furthermore, you're sending a clear and powerful signal that you value them and their contributions to the successes achieved within your four walls.

I mentioned that I've worked in and managed several nationally branded quick-service restaurants. Once there was a manager working in a restaurant who gave the opening-shift manager a time schedule according to which she had to complete all opening duties, but the shift manager could never complete the duties in the allotted time. When the general manager questioned her about her inability to complete all required tasks before opening, she answered that she needed another person so she could complete all the tasks.

Leading by example, instead of yelling or disciplining the shift manager, the general manager scheduled herself for an opening shift with the same personnel and resources normally available to the shift manager. Needless to say the general manager could not complete all the scheduled tasks. After the hands-on assessment, the general manager went to the shift manager, reported her findings, and then apologized for having set expectations that could not be met. She then provided her with the proper resources to meet those expectations. This is clearly a leader who understands that just giving directions, forcing situations, and not listening to input from her management and team members can trample the morale of the team, cause unnecessary turnover, and degrade the restaurant's customer-service experience. This manager understands that people are valuable and are her greatest asset.

A leader's interest in his or her personnel should not be confined within the four walls. If you're conscious of the fact that you're nothing without your personnel, why wouldn't you respect their personal schedules, private time, family commitments, and personal and professional goals? As the general manager, when you do respect such things, you're saying to each employee, "I value you as a person and a teammate."

Remember, these are just examples. Please feel free to apply this principle to all issues that occur with your employees—your greatest assets.

Let's advance this concept of valuing time a step further. General managers know what days they'll work, what days they'll be off, and when they want their vacations. Nothing within their four walls restrains their ability to execute or adjust their plans. But employees aren't always so lucky. Most ineffective leaders are arbitrary and unconcerned about doing things to help their employees manage their lives. Many will fail to post employee schedules on time, change schedules every week, schedule employees when they have properly requested for days off, and give them the third degree when they have an unplanned, but important, event in their lives that requires an empathetic management response. How is this respecting your employee's time? In reality, the behavior of the general manager only leads to high turnover and poor restaurant performance. Remember, the team's performance is highly responsive and reflective of your leadership, for better or worse.

In another case, there was a manager who led an inner-city quick-service restaurant in an extremely challenging environment. The restaurant had bulletproof glass, employees had to speak to customers through a speaker and pass the customer orders through a turnstile window. Talk about potential service barriers! However, at this restaurant this level of personal and physical security was a necessity due to the gang and drug activity in the area. As a side note, any quick-service brand that voluntarily accepts the challenge to provide its products and services to a community, despite its unique challenges, deserves praise, and if the situation is handled properly, the community will show its appreciation. The restaurant in this example did three million dollars in sales per year—consistently. Yes, selling fast food!

You're probably running the numbers by now and concluding that this manager, in an urban area, probably made approximately $10,000 in bonuses every quarter by maximizing profits through growing sales. When the manager was asked how the restaurant was successful, her answer was that she focused on her current and future employees. When pressed for a more detailed explanation, the manager revealed that she made strategic hires from the neighborhood by building relationships with customers and, through those relationships, discovering people in the neighborhood who had goals to enhance their futures. She didn't just wait for the applicants to present themselves; she formulated a hiring strategy within her four walls that was responsive to the environment.

Hiring people with personal goals beyond simply earning a paycheck for today's vanishing needs lays a foundation for a win-win relationship, and it eliminates employee behaviors upfront that conflict with the cultural norms within the four walls and those of the customer.

Another side note: so many times leaders stereotype their customers, assuming they represent the ills of the community. That alone will reveal itself in the team's indifferent attitude toward customers and will serve as a catalyst to stagnant sales growth and poor customer relations. Although the restaurant was in a challenged area, the manager made it a point to hire people from the neighborhood who could relate to the guests in a wowing manner.

The manager also shared a second practice: set people up for success from day one. Once you hire the people, you put them on the path to success through orientation and training. A conscious decision to bypass orientation and training is a decision to have subpar service, poor and inconsistent quality, and high turnover. Further, this manager said, "You have two chances to set expectations with employees: on orientation day and then on training days." The manager also believed setting and communicating goals with new hires was as important as telling them when and where to pickup their paychecks.

A third step relates to new hires and current employees. There is a biblical principle that says, "Without a vision people perish." The same principle applies to leading within the four walls. Obviously, general managers receive the brand's vision and mission from corporate leadership and through operational policies. However, while being true to that corporate vision, it's imperative for managers to build a vision tailored to the operations within their four walls. If you don't know and believe in the vision of your brand, you're destined to fail, and you're taking your team off the cliff with you. Remember, they're learning from your example. Furthermore, you're breeding a team that's indifferent and lacking in loyalty. If this attitude is allowed to fester, it will be a significant cancer in the organization and could potentially destroy the brand. This manager said she placed a high priority on getting her team on board with the company's and manager's visions and goals. The manager scheduled one-on-one meetings with each employee and junior manager to communicate these items. In the same meeting, she asked five personal and business questions and allowed each employee to ask five questions. Hers were:

1. Do you have siblings?
2. What are your hobbies?
3. What are your educational goals?
4. What are your career goals?
5. What are your expectations in working here?

Each meeting ended with her seeking the employee's commitment by asking if she could count on his or her involvement in improving the performance of the restaurant.

The manager explained that the benefit of the individual meetings is to gain commitment, because the internal team has to believe they have a stake in the operations and performance of the restaurant. Showing that you care about your employees is closely tied to their active participation in achieving the vision, and it will ultimately heighten the external customer experience.

As a testament to the positive influence a former leader or mentor can have on a manager, this manager said her previous manager taught that people were a restaurant manager's greatest asset and that to be successful you have to understand the concept of people. It's impossible to be an effective leader within your four walls if you don't understand how to lead people. This is something that comes from work experience, reading books, your own experiences, and, most of all, asking questions of and observing other great leaders.

To be successful within your four walls you must understand that employees who work with you will make or break you. If you don't have a leadership style that will put employees first, you can kiss long-term success good-bye.

It's frustrating as the general manager to get a customer complaint, fail an inspection, or miss targets, especially if it occurred on your day off. But you have to first ask yourself this question: "Have I earned the respect of my employees, and have they bought into the vision and goals enough to, in my absence, personally want to carry on the methods, values, and service priorities that I hold and display?" When looking at how you treat your employees can you honestly and undoubtedly say you're being successful because you understand your employees are your greatest assets?

Exercise: Answer these questions.
Within your four walls:

1) Is your turnover below 100 percent?
2) Do you value your employee's? If so, how do they feel it?
3) Are the schedules posted on time?
4) Do the employee's schedules change every week?
5) Are you consistent in orientation?
6) Do you provide adequate training?

Chapter Two

Leadership Within Your Four Walls

Leadership within your four walls starts with setting the example, role modeling, and illustrating what you expect from your employees. As the general manager, you're planning, organizing, and directing the operations activities and performance of your employees. You're influencing the behaviors of your employees and laying the foundation so that bottom line projections are met or exceeded. When a restaurant is consistently hitting sales and profits, it's not a fluke and it's not because the restaurant is the corporate golden child. The cause of a restaurant's success is likely the restaurant manager's effective leadership in planning, organizing, directing operational activities, holding all who work with the manager accountable for their actions, and doing all this intuitively. Don't breeze past the term intuitively. When a general manager has an unwavering commitment to using the corporate playbook (operations manual), leading the charge to provide extraordinary service and superior quality products by design, leading in training and development for himself or herself and the entire team, and implementing a predetermined method to assess, inspect, and improve every operation within their four walls, the result is consistently high performance. Actually, what's achieved is more than consistency. Because of the general manager's insistence on doing it right all day, every day, in training, in practice, during routine operations, through planned or unannounced assessments, in a good or bad economy, the behaviors become natural. They're as ordinary as breathing, walking, blinking. They happen without thought—subconsciously.

The exact opposite will occur when leadership within the four walls is indifferent, inconsistent, and incoherent. Where's the proof? Every time you run numbers for product cost, profits, service response times, customer complaints, etc., the warning signs are screaming loud and clear. Declining sales and profits are only symptoms of what's happening within the four walls of your restaurant.

Imagine working for someone who hasn't given you the slightest idea of what they expect of you or what his or her priorities are. It's like getting a first-round draft pick in a sports lottery, drafting a star, bringing them onto the team, and telling them to "get out there and play!" You haven't shared with them your coaching philosophy, goals, objectives, or explained the team's culture. Most importantly, you haven't bothered to give them the team's play book that's been flagged with the coach's comments. This type of toxic leadership will create disarray within your four walls. Everybody's doing whatever they think is best in their own minds. When that happens, once-enthusiastic and caring employees become dissatisfied and begin to second-guess their choices of employer and, in some instances, their career choices. Their dissatisfaction rolls downhill out of control into a huge negative snowball wiping out everything in its path: service, quality, morale, internal and external customer goodwill, you name it! Your lack of consistent, visible, and engaged leadership within your four walls caused it. Stop blaming your employees, the corporate office, your home life, the neighborhood where you're located, the high-maintenance customer with so-called unreasonable demands, and all the other creative excuses you have convinced yourself are legitimate. Just stop it! Stop whining and start leading within your four walls. When you get it together and start leading from the heart with some passion, commitment, and fortitude, everything and everyone will come together too! You'll see an immediate positive transformation within your four walls; I guarantee it!

I'll be the first to acknowledge that quick-service restaurant operations are a challenge because no two hours, two days, or two customers are the same. Sometimes it seems like you're playing Whac-A-Mole. Just when you think you've got all the moles mashed, another pops up—and then another—and then another. As frustrating as that may sound, you can actually win the game if you keep pounding. Be patient, but have a sense of urgency, learn the patterns and routines, know when to speed up or slow down, and have fun. Like the great leader Winston Churchill said: "Will never surrender!" It's important that your employees not only understand who the leader is but also what the leader expects within the four walls of your restaurant.

I'm reminded of a manager who worked for a nationally branded quick-service restaurant for sixteen years. She started as a team member, was identified as a promising future manager, and was promoted through various levels of management. She was happy working with the company. It provided great training and development and had ample advancement opportunities. However, after sixteen years of excellent service with the brand, she quit and took her skills to another quick-service restaurant. Now, before I give the details, I must tell you, do not do the Evelyn Woods thing and speed-read past this section, because you're going to really be surprised with what comes next. Let's see why the manager quit. She didn't leave the company because she was dissatisfied with advancement opportunities or because the company culture was not exemplary or because of a lack of properly placed policies and standards. The brand had all of those things and was committed to living, existing, and operating by them. This person left because of a miscarriage of leadership above her! Her immediate supervisor that represented the company did not set a good example for what the company was trying to achieve. The supervisor didn't seem to understand the basic premise that to be successful in quick-service restaurants, the leader's team had to believe the leader was trying with every resource available to follow the company's mission of putting people first. This senior manager was great at the dog and pony show when corporate executives visited the restaurant, but once the tour was over it was back to business as usual; leadership evaporated when the show ended. The accolades were given to the senior manager, not the restaurant manager or the restaurant team, and the spotlight was turned off. Clearly, this senior manager didn't lead by example, and life was unbearable for anyone who was committed to the brand's mission and vision. Corporate leadership bought the show hook, line, and sinker. There was nowhere to go except out. If you choose to exhibit

LEADERSHIP WITHIN YOUR FOUR WALLS

false leadership, you'll loose your best potential managers and your best team members.

Jim Collins wrote a book titled Good to Great. In it he wrote about getting the wrong people off the bus and the right people on it. In this scenario, the wrong people were getting off the bus because the wrong leadership was driving the bus into oncoming traffic at high-speed. Aren't you glad you didn't skip this section?

Let's look briefly about the quick-service world that's bustling right outside your four walls. All restaurants have competitors in their demographic area. You have competitors from your brand too! This will not come as a surprise to general managers who engage in self-driven competition within their four walls. But for those managers who think their competitor is only the "other guys," read on.

A person who knows my insatiable commitment to quality product and world-class customer service confided in me. He said, "Carolyn, I refuse to go to the fast-food restaurant (he gave the actual name of the national brand) that's right down the street from my house. The employees are mean, the place is always dirty, you never know if they'll have the items you want or if they'll prepare them properly, and when you talk to the manager about a problem, you immediately get the feeling nothing will change. You know what?

Nothing ever changed. But because I'm hopelessly addicted to their menu, I drive across town to their better and more dependably operated location. Sad, but very true."

So, what's my point? Your own brand is also your competition. By corporate marketing strategy, they aren't supposed to be, but when you aren't leading within your four walls (but the brand itself remains the public's favorite choice for whatever they are selling), people will skip over your location and drive out of their way to a better location.

Now, let's get back to our discussion about the quick-service world that is bustling right outside your four walls.

Do you wonder why some restaurants are busy during lunch and dinner and others are not? In any given geographic area, all quick-service restaurants are comparable. The only difference may be the products. The prices may vary but are in the same range. However, some quick-service restaurants in close proximity to yours are growing in sales, attracting the best workers, and improving their operations daily. And there are other restaurants that are inconsistent in their ability to drive transactions that grow sales. In those locations, customer traffic grinds to a nonsustainable rate. Eventually those restaurants close because of those conditions or because of the sheer poor management within the four walls and the never-ending, although good intentioned, false starts by concerned leadership to make midcourse corrections. Leading with intentionality and having an authentic concern for your team will prevent this from ever being your scenario.

There is no secret to being a successful restaurant leader, no universal leadership style or personality trait, and no one management philosophy. However, all restaurants have one thing in common: they all have people! The differences between high-performing, mediocre, and failing restaurants can be traced back to the restaurant's leadership and how they lead the people within their four walls.

Restaurants have internal customers. They're the people who work with you to achieve the established mission and vision of the brand. How the internal customers feel about your leadership, for better or worse, will directly and immediately influence the experience of your external customers. Whether that experience is positive or negative depends on your leadership within your restaurant's four walls.

To ensure that experience is positive, you have to walk the talk. As the leader within your four walls, letting your walk match your talk is important. If your goal is to increase sales, profits, and your personal net worth by earning bonuses and other financial rewards, you first must focus on the leadership within the four walls of the restaurant. Leading by example is one of the main methods and lowest cost resources you have at your disposal to influence others. If setting the example is not on the top of your list, then failure is! Today's generation of workers demands considerate interactions and reciprocal respect from their leaders. They watch every move the leader makes and only superficially listen to what the leader is saying, as David Cottrell states in Walk the Talk. Employees of today won't perform at a high level if they don't connect with the leader. I once heard someone say, "I can't hear what you're saying because what I see you doing is overpowering my ability to hear you!" When your walk and talk are in sync, people take pleasure in hearing, seeing, and following you. Walk the talk!

For example, there was a manager who disciplined an employee for being late to work and periodically taking unplanned days off by calling when they were supposed to be at work. Strangely, the manager himself had established a shift start time of 10:00 a.m. but consistently arrived anywhere from fifteen minutes to an hour late, thereby leaving the restaurant understaffed. When he'd arrive to work, he would give the shift manager a litany of reasons for his late arrival: "I needed to take care of personal business before reporting to work." or "I got stuck on a call with corporate (usually followed by some negative comments about corporate leadership)." or "I had car trouble."

When the manager disciplined the employee, of course the employee objected that it wasn't fair. "You come to work late every day," he told the manager. "And the other managers complain because when you aren't here we have to pick up the slack."

Before you take the position that rank has its privileges, consider the brand's operations policies and human resources guidelines. I don't believe you'll find it stated anywhere, "This policy applies to everyone except you." There are leadership and management roles that have flexible schedules and nontraditional time-and-place arrangements; however, a single unit restaurant manager's schedule is not likely one of those flex assignments.

Quick side bar: you should have a predictable schedule augmented with an unpredictable stop-in-to-see-how-things-are-going element. The reasons for this are obvious.

Now back to the late employee issue. As you see, the employee, consciously or not, was mirroring and following the leader's example. When you fail to hold yourself to the same standard that you have for your employees in similar circumstances, then you're the root cause of the performance deficiency. You failed to lead by example.

I know you're saying, "It's not the team member's responsibility to police a general manager's actions." I will emphatically disagree with you! Shocked? You shouldn't be. You should want them to watch you. Who best models excellence, character, integrity, responsibility, world-class customer service, anger-management, teamwork, recognition, brand mission execution, and vision embracing? The general manager is the best model, or should be.

As the leader, something as simple as coming to work late and expecting those who report directly to come to work on time will lead to poor operations, which in turn will lead to declining sales and profits. Role modeling the behavior that is expected of your employees will only accelerate the restaurant toward becoming a high-performing quick-service powerhouse.

On the other hand, there was another manager who demanded everyone's uniform be wrinkle-free, shirts tucked in, nametags worn and visible, and that they wear work shoes and dark socks. The manager had a meeting with his team in which he communicated verbally and visibly the expected uniform appearance. Furthermore, the manager stated that no employees were to come behind the counter or start their shifts unless their uniforms were complete. He went on to explain the consequences of not achieving excellence in this area. The leader also told the employees that the same standards required of them would be required of managers, including him. No one was exempt. So if team members observed a manager coming behind the counter in an incomplete uniform, they had the right to respectfully and appropriately bring the issue to the manager's attention without fear of retaliation.

They were given directions on how to execute such an unorthodox measure. This type of leadership empowered employees and quickly earned their respect. Because the management team was a solid, cohesive unit that led in upholding the dress standard, no manager was ever called out over his or her dress. In fact, it became a friendly challenge within the four walls to see who kept the best uniforms between the employees and the management team. As you can see, it's not enough to communicate your expectations, it's imperative to live what you expect and follow up on a daily basis to reinforce your guidelines. Role modeling the example is the only thing that will influence others. It's impossible to be successful within the four walls of your restaurant if you lack the ability to walk the talk.

When a leader does not lead by example, it will have a boomerang effect. For example, as in the case of the attendance issue we previously covered, the leader's own attendance practices will create the very conditions that give rise to employee tardiness and absenteeism. In the extreme alternative, it can lead to employees quitting their jobs. Regardless of what the manifestations are, ultimately such managerial behavior could lead to poor employee morale, high turnover, and declining sales.

Observe any restaurant that's consistently increasing its sales and profits year after year. You will inevitably find a general manager who's consistent in leadership and committed to leading by example within the four walls.

Here are some characteristics of a manager who provides leadership within his or her four walls:

- Believes in setting up everyone on the team for success
- Provides a stable environment
- Properly executes standards, procedures, and policies
- Uses established processes for hiring, training, and employee development
- Ensures proper food handling and safety
- Maintains a clean and occupationally safe restaurant environment for employees and customers
- Provides timely and appropriate performance feedback
- Ensures that adequate materials and resources are consistently available to operate the restaurant
- Follows the brand's operational guidance
- Models operational excellence, infectious ambition, and world-class service
- Serves as a leadership development incubator from which corporate can select future leaders
- Publicly recognizes expected performance by employees

Leadership Within Your Four Walls

Restaurant managers who accept responsibility for leading within their four walls are leaders who influence the behavior of their teams, develop managers, and hold employees and junior management accountable. These leaders will look into the mirror before addressing issues and confirm within themselves that they've held themselves to the highest standards in the areas they're addressing. They're willing to be transparent with regard to their shortcomings, and they model self-correction to their staffs. If you haven't figured it out yet, leadership isn't for cowards!

Leaders who understand these principles will never give away their power to lead and influence by being inconsistent in their leadership within the four walls of their restaurants. Giving your power away is equivalent to taking the battery out of your car and giving it to your neighbor. Every time you want to drive the car, you have to go next door and ask the neighbor's permission to use the battery to start it. It was your battery power from the start! Every time you have to correct an employee for an infraction that you also make, it's like having to ask for your own power back. This is a major violation and failure of leadership.

As the general manager, you're always being watched for your actions and behavior. When you're in the restaurant, whether visiting or on duty, you're still the general manager, and your actions matter. When you're on the premises and you don't bat an eye as you walk past incorrect product-hold times, incorrect execution of operations procedures, rude service, or violations of uniform appearance policies, you have loudly and clearly announced what the real policies and standards are within your four walls. The greater problem and loss of respect for your leadership comes when, all of sudden, the district manager drives up and you morph into manager par excellence. Now everything's important to you, even though you've just given up your power as the leader within your four walls. The urgency to perform as a leader only occurred because the district manager arrived. So the resulting message to the employees is that following procedures only matters if higher management visits the restaurant, but it's not important that it will demonstrate a commitment to the vision of the brand and the general manager or that it will support growth in sales by creating a buzz about your restaurant that attracts more customers who will continue to frequent the restaurant.

Great restaurant leaders are those who are consistent in their leadership roles and model appropriate actions and behaviors. They do it because leaders understand that success within their four walls is all about perception of the internal and external customers. Those leaders demand excellence from their team and in their operations, because the brand and its customers deserve the best service and product delivery at all times. They also know it's their actions as leaders that will provide the model for their teams.

Let's see what the impact will be within the four walls when the cat's away. Will the old adage prevail? In this scenario, a manager knew in advance that corporate was visiting in the area on a particular day. The day happened to be the manager's regular day off. His response to that information was quite the opposite of what most managers would have done. Not only did he not change his day off, he also didn't notify the managers on duty to expect a visit from the executive team. Blasphemy! This was surely career suicide in the making. Or was it? Well, the executive team did visit the restaurant and the feedback was great. In fact, the executive team had the area manager call and ask the general manager to come to the restaurant, not stating why but the executive team wanted to provide recognition to the general manager for great operations in his absence.. Well, what do you think? Was the general manager committing career suicide, or did he know he had a high-performing team trained to deliver consistently high-quality service and product anytime, any day, with and without the leader's presence, because the customers deserved it? You guessed it, it was like any other day within the manager's four walls and he simply continued on a successful career trajectory. This is because he knew the value of leading by example and investing in and benefiting from the churning and pain of training and developing the team. Additionally, and without argument, the manager positively exercised his power within the four walls of the restaurant because the standards were set by him, not by corporate visitors, through role modeling the expected behavior at all times and by everyone.

How many managers can say their restaurants routinely provide the best service and highest quality products regardless of which manager is on duty and without the threat of some impending assessment, cutback, or organizational shake-up? Not many. Leading by example is all about your actions while you're within the four walls of your restaurant, and it extends even further when you show the team you trust them by allowing them to stand on their own before external auditors in your absence. The elation and satisfaction that your team will have as a result of your leading by example, training and developing, holding high performance standards, and creating a family within your four walls can't be given a price tag. However, the emotional connection to the team, the vision, and the brand become amalgamated along with their self-confidence and self-actualization. You and your team can have this type of performance as a daily reality. And you can have the sales, career advancement, bonus check, and accolades to match. It all begins with choosing to lead and undergirding that choice with a commitment to leading by example.

I know there is somebody reading this book and saying, "I think under the right circumstance, these things are possible." If that's you, keep reading. If that's not you, also keep reading so you can share this story with someone who you think feels the same way. There was a manager in the western United States who took over a restaurant that was failing on all targets set by the company. Turnover was extremely high. The restaurant was doing $19,000 in sales per week in an area where the sales should have been in excess of $30,000 per week. Instead of approaching this new position like a bull in a china shop, she chooses to take a more methodological approach. Here's how she addressed the shortcomings in the restaurant.

First, the manager decided not to go into the restaurant to find underperforming employees and terminate them. According to her philosophy, the employees were valuable assets. She believed in people and did not believe that employees get up and come to work just to bring the restaurant down. This leader believed that, except in extreme situations, leadership dictates how a person performs at work.

With this in mind, the leader decided that in the first thirty days she was going to lead mostly by example, to model what her expectations were, and also to earn the respect of the team by demonstrating that she was not only a competent leader but a team player who could effectively work every position in the restaurant. Through this approach, during the first thirty days she corrected many critical issues. At the same time she observed and took notes on all other issues. While letting her actions show the team the expectations she has for running successful operations, the manager was simultaneously earning respect as the leader of the restaurant. This is important, because the average manager would have gone into a new environment demanding respect through intimidation, which seldom gets long-term results. When your actions (walk) match your talk, a team will gladly follow your lead. However, any inconsistency in your leadership will cause a decline in power and influence as the leader within the four walls. This manager knew that leading by example, correctly following processes, and accepting complete responsibility for the restaurant as it stands, for better or worse equals a team that would voluntarily follow her lead and yield a substantial growth in sales and profits.

It's time to be honest about your ability to lead. Here are a few clues to use to assess whether or not you're an effective leader:

- Your leadership (adjusted for the situation) works in any demographic area.

- You're able to grow sales regardless of the location.
- You continuously have low turnover.
- Your restaurant runs efficiently.
- Your restaurant team consistently achieves breakthrough results on evaluations.
- You're delivering the expected profit margins.

If you're doing at least these things, then you're a consistent leader and are likely modeling the appropriate behavior found in high-performing teams. However, if you're challenged by this list and by the idea of turning an underperforming restaurant around within six months, you must look in the mirror, be honest with yourself about your leadership, and make a change. Leadership and excellence within your four walls are not beyond your reach. You just have to want it, do what it takes to achieve it, and share the success with your team. Leadership is walking the talk. So stop talking and start walking, and before you know it, you'll glance over your shoulder and find a trail of employees following in your footsteps.

Exercise: Have an open mind, answer the questions, and then take action!

1) What actions are causing your team to follow your lead in a positive or negative manner?
2) What do you think you should continue doing in your leadership?
3) What do you think you should stop doing?
4) What do you think you should change about your leadership?

Chapter Three

Accountability and Responsibility Within Your Four Walls

Having control of your restaurant is an important aspect of being a general manager. Control means having accountability and responsibility for performance within the four walls of your restaurant. As high-performing managers, we are driven to achieve competitive product cost targets without compromising product quality or product availability. Taking it a step further, we want to have the tightest labor targets without operational inefficiency or compromises in customer service. Finally, we have an almost insatiable desire to develop others to become the future leaders in the restaurant, the brand, and possibly even in the quick-service industry. However, sometimes, because of all the fires that blaze within our four walls, seemingly out of control at times, it's easy to become blinded to the root cause of most recurring issues, many of which were minor or insipient concerns when first discovered. Without realizing it, even high-performing leaders sometimes blame others or find themselves in denial about the waning performance of usually high-performing restaurants.

It would be dishonest to fail to acknowledge that being accountable for every inch within your four walls, twenty-four hours a day, seven days a week, 365 days a year is a scary thought. No manager wants to accept the responsibility for a declining restaurant, a low-performing location, or a previous manager's mess. It certainly would be easy, and almost justifiable, to say it's not your fault that the restaurant failed the health inspection or is dirty, that product costs are too high, that there's too much employee turnover, that customer complaints are too high, etc. It's tempting to want to distance yourself from current negative conditions. However, as unfair as it may feel, the reality is that if you've been the leader of the restaurant for more than six months and significant problems still exist, then you're responsible, and the situation requires your immediate attention.

As the manager of everything within the four walls of your restaurant, the first step to becoming successful is being accountable and responsible for all actions and activities of the team. Yes, you're accountable for the good, the bad, and the ugly during your time as a restaurant manager, regardless of whether or not you're on shift. The team you lead is a reflection of your leadership. Successful managers acknowledge that.

For example, if asked, "Why is the restaurant missing sales compared to last year?" the average manager will blame the economy, advertising, the location of the restaurant, new competition in the area, product selections, or high prices. But in truth, it's because of the manager's leadership. He or she is accountable and responsible for what happens within those four walls.

I know a manager who took over a restaurant that was making $800,000 per year. The location was at a busy intersection and had fierce competition on each corner from other national brands, including one selling the same basic product. There were also three restaurants of the same brand within two miles. Now, mind you, this store had been consistently underperforming for at least fifteen years, but that all changed with the assignment of this new manager.

Six months after she took over this restaurant, the sales volume had increased from $15,000 per week to $30,000 per week, and for the first time in fifteen years the restaurant was blazing a trail to join the million-dollar sales club on that highly competitive corner and within the brand. You're probably saying this is an unbelievable tale. Believe it. This is a true and accurate story.

How did she do it? The first thing she did was acknowledged that it was now her restaurant; she accepted the responsibility and held herself accountable for its performance. She didn't pay attention to the horror stories or the goliath competitors outside her four walls. She simply turned her focus to within her four walls, developed a plan of action, and fiercely implemented it with the help of her team, ensuring her daily activities and actions correlated with growing sales. Boom! A million-dollar restaurant emerged among the so-called quick-serve behemoths.

A major difference between this manager and her predecessors was that they let the restaurant run them instead of them running the restaurant. If you want to follow her lead in a similar situation, instead of playing the victim card and allowing the same performance to continue on a daily basis, take control and align the restaurant's daily activities around what you're trying to accomplish. This manager had a goal to increase sales, so she stepped back and observed what was actually hindering sales on a daily basis. She explored the financial status, the customer service, and the activities of the employees and managers. She monitored the quality of the product being served and the expressions on the faces of the internal and external customers. During the exploring stages, the manager found the restaurant was losing over $5,000 per month in cash losses, the food costs were 8 percent out, and the store was overusing labor to the tune of 150 hours per month. The manager found there were no processes in place to maintain a clean environment. Additionally, following the lead of a mentor and quick-service restaurant giant, she spent many hours in the lobby observing customer service and talking to the customers. The lobby activity was the most interesting to her.

The manager observed customers asking for freshly cooked product or inquiring if product was available today. She observed customers checking their bags for accuracy before walking out the door. And she found that the average service time was approximately ten minutes per customer. Are you seeing the issues here? When your customers can't trust their orders to be packed with fresh food—or even worse, with the correct food—and when they have to wait ten minutes for that kind of sketchy service, it won't be long before you see them visiting your competition on the corner.

What do you think about the following scenario? To understand it, you must put yourself in the customer's shoes. You're hungry, short on time, and probably a little preoccupied, too. To quell those hunger pangs, you go to your favorite quick-service restaurant. The service is great and fast (woo hoo!), but when you get in your car and back in gridlocked traffic, your taste buds are firing on all cylinders and you're now ready to eat your food. You reach into your bag with great anticipation of enjoying all the heavenly flavors only to discover the order is wrong or incomplete. I can't write what words would actually come out of your mouth, but you can imagine them, because you've probably been in that situation at one point or another. The real question is, what is the value in serving crappy food fast? Or what good is it to serve a properly prepared entrée that's hot when the other items in the order are cold because they were packaged before the main entrée was ready.

The manager continued the quest and walked the outside of the building, observing and noting what customers see when they drive into the parking lot—you know, the curb appeal. Believe it or not, a customer gives a restaurant several chances, starting with the parking lot, the outer limits of your four walls.

True story: A customer called the brand's complaint line to say there were weeds around the drive-through speaker (yes, weeds in the landscaping). She vowed never to visit that restaurant again. See how important the curb appeal is? The slightest issue may contribute to losing sales, because there are many customers with different priorities, satisfaction triggers, or pet peeves that will turn them away from your restaurant.

The manager observed graffiti on portions of the building, old grease stains and excessive trash around the Dumpster, and a drive-through menu board that was unorganized, missing lights and covered in water spots. The windows at the doors had excessive fingerprints, and the trash was overflowing in the lobby.

Side bar. Customers give you three chances before making a decision to purchase your product. They note if the parking lot is clean, if the windows clean, and if the lobby is clean. If you strike out on all three, you've lost a customer.

The next step the manager took was to observe the procedures in the kitchen. There she found that the cooks were not properly following the preparation procedures nor using the tools to maintain quality product correctly. Lastly, the she observed all the managers running their shifts (yes, I mean invested time in visiting every manager's shift) so that she could avoid making assumptions and jumping to conclusions regarding their management methods and results. The manager identified opportunities for improvement in each manager's ability to control a floor and found the restaurant was controlling the managers. A simple thing such as a cashier needing change in the middle of a rush was a problem; not having change interrupts the flow of the customers and cashier. Instead of managers being proactive by giving rounds of change before the rush, they took the risk of allowing the cashiers to determine their needs and ask for change. Even then managers only gave change to cashiers who asked for it and only the amount they asked for. So managers could easily have been asked for change again in five minutes or, even worse, in the middle of a rush. As mentioned before, if the manager would have been proactive and given enough change to all cashiers before the rush the manager would have eliminated service bottlenecks. The new general manager noticed these simple but critical issues as she observed junior managers controlling the floor.

Haunted by the sense of urgency to get the restaurant on a winning path, average managers would not have taken the time to observe the operations, talk to the customers, or work with each manager. Instead they would have glanced at these issues and jumped into the blazing fire. Eventually they would have been burned because they would have become part of the fire, and they'd have had no plan on how to extinguish it. Average managers might have thought the best solution was to blame the current team members for their lack of skills or will to operate with excellence, and they might have decided to make a costly decision to terminate the old crew and hire a new team. This is the greatest mistake a manager makes when taking over a restaurant. Whether the restaurant is run well or poorly, the manager needs people who are willing to work with him or her. The only way to achieve alignment is by being a caring and principled manager who leads by example, sets controls, and earns the team's respect instead of demanding it. Let the respect happen naturally.

Successful leaders of quick-service restaurants analyze the talent of their employees. They attempt to show them consistent leadership and give them an opportunity to mirror and demonstrate acceptable behaviors and actions before deciding to terminate individuals or the entire team. A new manager who's shortsighted may tell him or herself, "This is not my team. I didn't hire them, and therefore I won't take responsibility for their actions." This attitude will result in the loss of the current team. Many team members will leave by their own choosing. All the while the fires continue to blaze, the restaurant continues to struggle with no appreciable improvement, and eventually the new manager is removed or quits.

The high-performing manager who took over this low performing restaurant understood that the first step to turning a restaurant around is accepting responsibility and accountability for its current state. After doing that, she prioritized the issues and decided that the first task was to find what was stopping the restaurant from experiencing sales growth within its four walls. She used mind mapping with sales as the target. Then she put all the issues she had observed around that target, categorized the issues, developed a plan, and put it into action.

As the leader, you need to embrace the issues and ask which leadership style will help institute appropriate controls that will turn your restaurant around as quickly as possible. When you're the restaurant manager for three months or more and still have inconsistencies in the operations, high turnover and declining sales, remain confident that the leadership you're providing will ultimately help you accomplish the goals and objectives you've set for the restaurant. When taking responsibility, the buck stops with you as the leader. Until you can say that your leadership influenced others' behaviors for the betterment of the restaurant, you must continue to strengthen how you lead. The manager of the western United States restaurant consistently stepped into the shoes of all positions in an effort to gain firsthand knowledge on how situations were occurring. Even though she was not the previous manager who allowed all of the operational issues, she took accountability.

For example, while observing the customers in the lobby, she saw that one was upset because she was missing a side dish from her order. The manager could have said, "I'm new at this location. Let me find out who packed the order or let me see your receipt." Instead, she apologized to the customer, went behind the counter, and corrected the problem. She then thanked the customer, introduced herself as the general manager, and assured the customer the problem would be corrected for the future. The manager made a note to address the problem with the customer service team. When taking responsibility for what goes on within your four walls, it's important to find root causes of problems. Don't blame others for doing their jobs incorrectly until you're sure they caused a problem by acting contrary to what they knew to be correct.

Managers are sometimes quick to find fault in others because it's the easy way out. However, experienced leaders take ownership of the performance of others and of issues that occur within the four walls of their restaurants. They then find long-term solutions to the problems they encounter.

The manager at the restaurant in the example did not cower from the problems and allow them to continue; she accepted the responsibility for them and held herself accountable. She knew it was her responsibility to grow sales and deliver profit and that it was under her control.

At this time, the manager decided from the mind map there were two obstacles to growing sales in this restaurant: the knowledge of her employees and their training. She decided that focusing on the training of all employees and managers would eliminate 90 percent of the issues in the restaurant.

When leaders are committed to driving great performance within the four walls of their restaurants, they understand being accountable and taking responsibility are the critical first steps toward making positive changes. In addition, they understand the knowledge and morale of their employees are the most important vehicles in the journey to success within the four walls. These leaders understand that with control of the restaurant, growing sales is inevitable.

Exercise: Answer these questions:

1) Are you achieving breakthrough sales and profits?
2) If not, what is your responsibility and accountability in becoming a high-performing leader within your four walls?
3) Do you hold yourself accountable for growing sales?
4) Are your actions and activities showing your subordinates that you're accountable and that you accept the responsibility for their growth and the performance of the restaurant?

Chapter Four

Training Within Your Four Walls

You must live and breathe the brand's vision and your own restaurant's vision if you want to achieve extraordinary results and lead high-performing teams, and you have to do the same with training and development. Specifically, you must believe in training. Throughout my years of working in the quick-service industry, I've found that every consistently successful quick-service business unit had this in common: the general manager vigorously believed in training and would do whatever it took to ensure every new and current employee received the full breadth and depth of the required training.

Knowing that, it's amazing to me when I come across managers who struggle with, circumvent, and short-circuit training requirements under the excuse of having to cover immediate and urgent operational imperatives. As a result of their error, when operational performance assessments, health department inspections, or any number of planned or impromptu audits or evaluations come up, managers consistently end up hoping and praying that their employees will somehow magically follow all procedures correctly. We often say, "Real life performance is reflective of training and preparation." Stated another way, performance is a replica of the training and development the leader of the restaurant provides to the employees on the front-end and on a daily basis.

Training is a perpetual activity that has a continuous and repeating cycle: train, do, assess, train, do, assess, etc. It has a beginning but not an end, because since change is constant, training is constant. When change ceases, the organism can be declared dead or simply obsolete. A wise leader knows training and development are essential to sustaining growth, expansion, and operational excellence within their four walls and throughout the brand.

There was a manager fresh out of training who was placed in a restaurant that just failed a corporate evaluation and would be reevaluated within the next thirty days. The area manager asked the new manager if he needed help from peers to prepare for the evaluation. The new manager, who was new not only to the restaurant but to the brand, said, "No, thank you. I need to learn more about the standards and procedures, and the best way to do that is by using my operations manual to prepare for the evaluation."

This manager also decided to retrain the team by having them watch him prepare all products using established procedures. He told the team members to provide feedback and corrections throughout the process. When in doubt about the steps the manager was taking, they were to read the procedures out loud. This was brilliant. He was training the team members and earning their respect at the same time.

The thirty days passed, and the evaluation was conducted. The restaurant passed with a score of 91 percent. This manager brought skills and knowledge from his previous job along with one major philosophy: he believed in training. He decided to get ready for the evaluation without the assistance of peers, not for reasons of arrogance or intraorganizational competition, but because he decided whatever they did to prepare for the evaluation would be the standards for running a high-performing restaurant. The holders of those standards needed to remain in the restaurant when the evaluation was completed. He was confident that peers would have gotten them through the evaluation, but once it was completed they would have returned to their own restaurants, and his restaurant would not have gained any real improvement within its four walls.

Leadership Within Your Four Walls

All managers want to be successful. The previous chapters talked about the fact that a manager's leadership style dictates his or her success within the four walls of the restaurant. Knowing and believing a well-trained team is your greatest asset should assist in shaping the leadership you provide within the four walls

Recall the manager who doubled the in-store sales within six months of taking charge of the restaurant. The customer-service issue was major, because without customers the restaurant would have declining sales in a demographic area where the sales should have been growing consistently. However, when customers can't depend on your restaurant to get the order correct, have fresh food available, and provide great hospitality on every visit, they will eventually make a choice to go across the street to the competitor, and so will your employees, because it's an embarrassment to work in a restaurant that can't satisfy the internal or external customers. Recall the order errors. To address the incorrectly packed orders, the manager stepped backed and asked questions of the team members and observed their activities and actions. She came to the conclusion that team members, too, were frustrated with the poorly operating restaurant. They were tired of having to negotiate with the customers because product was not available, condiments were not available, or the service was too slow. To remedy those frustrations, the manager decided to spend thirty days training new and old employees.

If you find yourself in a similar situation, the reason for the focus on both old and new employees, aside from the fact that if you choose to train one group or the other the problems would still exist, is that by only focusing on the new employees you'd be creating a potential difficult environment. Current employees would start to resent the new employees and you, their manager, and they might feel threatened. This could hinder your progress toward correcting operational issues and cause improvements to take longer, because the entire team would not be aligned and uniformly trained.

Although the new employees received training following the new-hire training schedule, this manager took a different route with the existing employees. She didn't treat them as new hires, because it would have demeaned them. Instead, she verified all current team members' standards by creating a training certification program. Once the manager observed and coached all of the more experienced team members, they received a certificate of their competence in a particular area. This process only took fifteen days. By investing the nine days in recertifying the entire team on all positions, the manager prevented team members from saying they weren't trained correctly. Now the manager had confidence that all employees were trained correctly. By doing the training from scratch, she was "killing the spider" to eliminate further issues with training (or the spider web from reappearing).

The manager was setting herself up for success within the four walls of her restaurant. She acknowledged that there were problems with hospitality, speed of service, product availability, and product quality. She had enough knowledge to know a manager can't correct customer service without first correcting the issues with product. So she started training in the area of ordering, then moved to storage, then preparation, then cooking, and finally the packaging of the menu items. Imagine coaching customer-service workers on hospitality, speed, suggestive selling, or packing product correctly if the actual issue with every other order is product quality. The customers and cashiers would continue to be frustrated, and the sales would continue to decline. You can make a choice to terminate the cashiers and start over, or you can make a decision to provide training to remove the cause of the problem. In this case, it was the kitchen.

Starting in the kitchen, the manager took control by tirelessly working with day and night shifts, observing the procedures, inserting training where needed and doing the famous modeling of wanted behaviors to guide kitchen staff practices. The manager spent five days in the kitchen earning the kitchen staff's respect by showing her skills and correcting their skills, teaching what was expected of the cooks at all times. The manager was inspiring the cooks to have pride and showing them they were the core of the restaurant and had an accountability and responsibility to the customers and cashiers to have fresh and properly prepared products available at all times. Once the manager completed the shoulder-to-shoulder training, she was confident the workers were properly aligned with the brand and manager's vision for kitchen operations. This sounds unreal, but once employees earn respect for their leader, the pride follows and will continue as long as the leader is in control within the four walls of the restaurant.

Remember, it's impossible to correct hospitality, speed, food, cost, or labor issues in a quick-service restaurant without a high-performing kitchen, and most customers come to a restaurant for the quality product and hospitality, and sometimes even the speed.

Once the issues with product were corrected, the manager was able to address the customer service issues. The manager spent seven working days monitoring the product and working in the front of the house, shoulder-to-shoulder with the cashiers. This became a simple fix, because the product was now consistently available, thus eliminating the issues with incorrect orders, courtesy, and speed of service. To sustain high-performing customer service, managers provided on-the-spot, spontaneous role-playing with the cashiers and consistently listened to how they were taking orders to eliminate any assumptions they held that were not aligned with the leaders' expectations.

The best part about this story is when the manager went back to the lobby to observe the customer's expressions and actions and the cashier's hospitality, she noticed a customer checking her bag. She approached the customer and kindly said, "I give you my guarantee that order is correct. We're glad you gave us the opportunity to serve you. Thank you, and please come back again."

The response was priceless, and the buzz about the restaurant began to spread. As you can see, this small but critical step in providing training and removing obstacles jump-started the restaurant's sales growth. See, this is not rocket science. Training will give you success that will last as long as you're the leader of this restaurant. The first step toward being a respected leader within the four walls of a restaurant is earning the team's trust and respect by providing impactful training and using the resources and tools at your disposal.

Exercise: Answer the questions:

1) How many people on your team today have received adequate training?
2) When was the last time you, as the leader, checked to see if your team members were executing procedures correctly?
3) What area of training do you need to improve to take your restaurant to the next level?

Chapter Five

Develop Managers Within Your Four Walls

Remember, we continue to remove the spider web, but it continues to return, so we sweep it away again and again, only to see it return. This is like our restaurant: we constantly coach, discipline, or change managers because the same problems continue to occur, like a spider web. But have you thought about killing the spider itself so the web does not return?

In this case, the spider is the problem. The managers who work with you will do a better job if you take the time to develop their skills! It doesn't matter if it's a crew chief, shift lead, second assistant manager, or first assistant manager—all will perform better once you take the time to train and develop them as future leaders. By now you know I tell stories about each situation. And remember, all of the stories are true, not fiction.

There are many successful restaurant managers through out the country. Over the years of working in the fast-food industry, I have witnessed successful managers who believe in mentoring and bringing others with them, because the more your managers know, the less stressful it is to be a general manager. Imagine a management team of five, and all of them are capable of being a general manager because of your leadership. Now, that's an accomplishment! Some general managers think developing their staff in this way is a mistake because such well-trained managers might replace them, but high-performing managers see this as being a great leader.

The manager in the earlier example who was successful in turning around a failing restaurant was eventually promoted to the next level. Her promotion was possible because her leadership consistently and reliably yielded results. This manager had the knowledge, skills and ability to be successful. Her priority was building capability within her team at all levels. Leading a restaurant team is most rewarding when you witness others being promoted because of your leadership. Leaders are influencers. They lead by example and enjoy developing others to become leaders. As a leader, you face many problems on a daily basis, and more often than not it's the same set of problems that keeps recurring. The general manager has an obligation to give the brand a return on its investment in the form of profit. When the restaurant is not making profit even when sales are growing, it's because the general manager has not developed his or her managers to think and act like business owners. It doesn't matter how well we train our team members if the manager on duty has no clue how to run a business efficiently. Until they do, you'll constantly be fighting fires.

For example, there was a manager who continued to struggle with making the food cost target, so the general manager would come in and look at the numbers. If the food cost target was missed, the general manager would call the closing manager and question his ability. Not once did the general manager break the cost down and figure out which products were causing the problem before making the call to the closing manager.

See, sometimes you can manage by intimidation and duress. The numbers will start showing targets being met, but for how long? In this case, after the general manager called the shift manager and yelled and threatened him, the next day the restaurant hit product cost. The general manager was happy but didn't question how, all of a sudden, the food cost was in line. Never questioning the integrity of the numbers is a problem waiting to happen. See, it's possible to have success, but at what cost when as the general manager you fail to develop your managers?

The product cost remained in line for a couple of months, so the general manager stopped harping on that issue, not noticing that sales were declining. But one day she did inventory and realized the numbers were not matching up. However, instead of finding the root cause, she met with the management team and provided some harsh coaching about taking inventory correctly. The numbers got back on track quickly. The area manager came to visit and was discussing the high deletes and daily inventory fluctuations. When discussing the problem, the general manager said, "The problem with food cost was addressed with the other managers, but it keeps recurring."

The area manager took the general manager through some questions on the steps taken to correct the problem, and the manager said she provided coaching several times. The area manager asked her if she observed each manager running his or her shift? Had she closed with each manager? Had she audited her financial paperwork (deletes, giveaways, employee meals, etc.)? The manager answered no to all of the questions.

The area manager said, "The problem with the food cost is that you haven't removed the problem [spider]; you've been providing symptomatic solutions through verbal coaching [removing the spider web] and not finding the root cause of the problem so you can develop your managers."

As restaurant leaders, you have an obligation to resolve problems through exploring and finding solutions that will remove the spider so the web will not return.

How about the manager who spends more time borrowing product than running the restaurant? For example, a restaurant ran out of a product because of inefficient ordering. When questioned by the general manager, it was found that all managers used the build-to process, but when one specific manager submitted orders, the store would run short on product. Instead of doing the orders with the manager, the general manager provided written coaching without asking questions about the manager's knowledge of using an order form. If the general manager had asked questions, he would have realized the manager didn't understand how to properly use the form. He could have eliminated a recurring problem.

Developing managers by building their capability to carry out all functions will earn the general manager respect within the four walls of the restaurant. The examples above are simple recurring problems, but consider all of the problems that occur on your day off. Consider the issues with consistently achieving customer targets, sales targets, profit targets, and turnover targets. If you would take the time to develop your managers, the investment would return success without compromising your integrity. In addition, the success would be for the long-term.

Remember, building the capability of your managers is more than saying, "Just fix it." It's about working shoulder-to-shoulder, stimulating their minds by asking questions, getting their ideas on how to correct problems, and providing adequate training on how to lead a shift on their own.

Leadership Within Your Four Walls

Exercise: Answer the questions:

1) When you're off, are you comfortable with any manager being in control of the restaurant?
2) When was the last time you worked shoulder-to-shoulder with a struggling manager?
3) Does your leadership role model the standards you expect your managers to follow?
4) Who have you developed to become the next leader of a restaurant in the last year?

Chapter Six

Reflections on Leadership Within Your Four Walls

Leading within the four walls of any quick-service restaurant is a challenge no matter how you view it. However, having a passion for people and the quick-service business will dictate your success as the leader of the restaurant. When a restaurant is not growing year-over-year sales, remember that missing sales targets is only a symptom of other issues within the four walls.

As the leader it's important you understand that you influence behavior, and regardless of the location of your restaurant or other challenges, you can be successful. When you empower your team and managers through training and developing, every day will be a rewarding day within your four walls.

Remember, customers will travel far to a restaurant that provides an exemplary experience. Your leadership and what you model will be what your team will imitate. If you're serious about standards, procedures, and policies so will the people who work with you be. Remember, you're the local ambassador representing the company or brand that you work with, and your employees see you as the executive of that brand within your four walls. So when employees are frustrated and dissatisfied with the brand, they're really frustrated and dissatisfied with you as a leader.

Be the leader within the four walls of the restaurant and you'll enjoy the career you've chosen in the quick-service industry. Yes comedians and others say degrading things about our profession, but we know working in the quick-service industry affords us stable and progressive careers in Fortune 50, 100, and 500 companies, as well as educational opportunities, home ownership, automobiles, vacations, retirement, and so much more! So be proud of the quick-service restaurant you've chosen to make your career with, take ownership of your restaurant, and believe that success is with the people who work with you. Believe in training, be consistent with your leadership, maintain control of the four walls of your restaurant, and lastly, develop your managers. Success is waiting for you, your managers, and your team within your four walls.

www.ingramcontent.com/pod-product-compliance
Lightning Source LLC
Chambersburg PA
CBHW071803170526
45167CB00003B/1151